I Know That!

Seashore and Tides

Claire Llewellyn

FRANKLIN WATTS
LONDON•SYDNEY

First published in 2005 by Franklin Watts
96 Leonard Street, London EC2A 4XD

Franklin Watts Australia
Level 17/207 Kent Street, Sydney NSW 2000

Series adviser: Gill Matthews, non-fiction literacy
*   consultant and Inset trainer*
Series editor: Rachel Cooke
Editor: Sarah Ridley
Series design: Peter Scoulding
Designer: Jemima Lumley

Acknowledgements: Leo Batten/FLPA 14; George Bernard/NHPA 6, 7, 22l; Laurie Campbell/NHPA 15b, 16; Carr Clifton/Minden Pictures/FLPA 19; Chris Fairclough cover, title page, imprint page, 11b, 13b, 22r, 23; Tim Fitzharris/Minden Pictures/FLPA 5; Jeff Goodman/NHPA 15t; Chinch Gryniewicz/Ecoscene 18; Angela Hampton/Ecoscene 17; Kevin King/Ecoscene 12; Alberto Nardi/NHPA 11t; National Trust Photo Library 8, 9, 21; Mark Newman/FLPA 4; Pierre Petit/NHPA 10; Paul Thompson/Ecoscene 20; Alan Williams/NHPA 13.

A CIP catalogue record for this book is available from the British Library.

ISBN: 0 7496 6367 7
Dewey decimal classification number: 577.69'9

Printed in Malaysia

Contents

Land and sea

The seashore is the place where the land meets the sea.

In some places the seashore is sandy.

There are cliffs and rocks along this seashore.

Have you ever visited the seashore? What did you do there?

What are tides?

Twice a day, the sea rises up the shore and drops back down again. This is called the tide.

At high tide, the sea covers the shore.

At low tide, the beach is much larger.

Have you ever built a
sandcastle at the seaside?
What happened to your castle
when the tide came in?

High tide, low tide

Some places look very different at high and low tide.

At high tide, there is an island off the seashore.

At low tide, you can walk along a path to the island.

Look carefully at the pictures. What can you see at low tide that you cannot see at high tide?

Plants on the seashore

Plants that live on the shore have special ways of surviving the Sun, the sea and the tides.

Sea holly has tough leaves that do not dry out in the salty air.

The roots of sea grass can hold onto sand.

What plants have you seen on the seashore?

Seaweed grips the breakwater. It can live a long time out of water.

Animals on the seashore

At high tide, some animals are covered by water. At low tide, they are out in the air.

Mussels and limpets cling to rocks. At low tide, their shells protect them from the Sun.

At low tide, birds hunt for worms and shellfish in the sand and mud.

Lugworms tunnel under the sand, leaving piles of sand like these behind them. Look out for them on the shore.

Rockpools

When the tide goes out on a rocky shore, it leaves pools of water behind.

Many plants and animals live in rockpools.

Starfish feed on mussels by opening their shells.

A sea anemone has tentacles to catch food.

Have you ever looked in rockpools? What did you find?

Washed up

Anything that floats in the sea may be washed up by the tide.

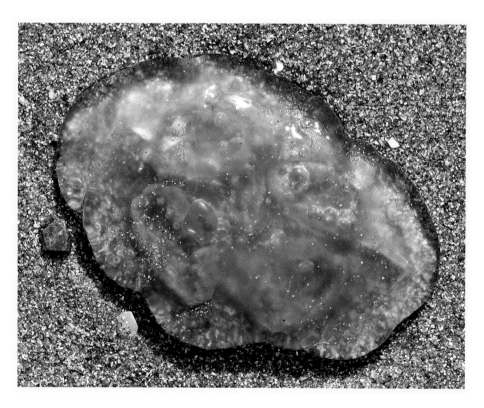

Stranded jellyfish dry out on the shore.

Many plastic bottles have washed up on this seashore. What else can you see?

Look out for shells on the seashore. Sea animals used to live inside them.

The changing shore

As the sea comes in and out, the seashore slowly changes.

Waves crash against the cliffs. Day by day, they crumble into rocks.

Rocks are worn down by the waves – first to pebbles, then into shingle, then into sand.

Pebbles are round and very smooth. Can you think why?

Protecting the seashore

The seashore is easily spoilt. It is important to protect it.

In summer, many people use the shore. Some leave their rubbish behind.

No one is allowed to change this seashore.

You can help protect the
seashore by always taking
your rubbish home.

I know that...

1 The seashore is the place where the land meets the sea.

2 The tides are the rise and fall of the sea.

3 The seashore can look different at high and low tide.

4 Seashore plants can survive the sea and the waves.

5 Many seashore animals can live in water or out of it.

6 On rocky shores, there are rockpools at low tide.

7 Many things are washed up by the tide.

8 The sea wears down cliffs into rocks. The rocks wear down into pebbles, and finally into sand.

9 We must all protect the seashore.

Index

About this book

I Know That! is designed to introduce children to the process of gathering information and using reference books, one of the key skills needed to begin more formal learning at school. For this reason, each book's structure reflects the information books children will use later in their learning career – with key information in the main text and additional facts and ideas in the captions. The panels give an opportunity for further activities, ideas or discussions. The contents page and index are helpful reference guides.

The language is carefully chosen to be accessible to children just beginning to read. Illustrations support the text but also give information in their own right; active consideration and discussion of images is another key referencing skill. The main aim of the series is to build confidence – showing children how much they already know and giving them the ability to gather new information for themselves. With this in mind, the *I know that...* section at the end of the book is a simple way for children to revisit what they already know as well as what they have learnt from reading the book.